ACTION SPORTS

RALLY CAR RACING

By K. A. Hale

Kaleidoscope
Minneapolis, MN

The Quest for Discovery Never Ends

This edition is co-published by agreement between Kaleidoscope and World Book, Inc.

Kaleidoscope Publishing, Inc.
6012 Blue Circle Drive
Minnetonka, MN 55343 U.S.A.

World Book, Inc.
180 North LaSalle St., Suite 900
Chicago IL 60601 U.S.A.

Kaleidoscope ISBNs
978-1-64519-067-7 (library bound)
978-1-64494-148-5 (paperback)
978-1-64519-168-1 (ebook)

World Book ISBN
978-0-7166-4360-9 (library bound)

Library of Congress Control Number
2019938879

Printed in the United States of America.

Bigfoot lurks within one of the images in this book. It's up to you to find him!

TABLE OF CONTENTS

CHAPTER 1

RACE UP MOUNT WASHINGTON

It is 2010. Travis Pastrana sits in his Subaru. Mount Washington looms over him. This mountain is in New Hampshire. Pastrana will drive up the Mount Washington Auto Road. He wants to beat the record time.

The Auto Road is 7.6 miles (12.2 km) long. It winds up the mountain. It's the tallest mountain in the northeast United States. The road twists and turns. There are parts with no rail. It's dangerous even at slow speeds. And Pastrana will be going fast.

In 2010, Travis Pastrana wanted to beat the record time racing up the Mount Washington Auto Road.

Pastrana's codriver sits next to him. His name is Marshall Clarke. The codriver has a big job. Rally racing doesn't happen on racetracks. Racers drive on public streets. The driver doesn't know what's coming. The codriver tells him what's ahead.

Clarke and Pastrana drove the road together yesterday. They drove at normal speed. Clarke took notes. He can't guide Pastrana the wrong way. They could go off a cliff.

He and Pastrana have come up with a code. This will help them **communicate** quickly.

Pastrana is ready. He sits at the starting line. Clarke counts him down. Go! They start up the mountain. Clarke gives him directions the whole way. They average 72 miles per hour (116 km/h). They use their code. Clarke uses numbers. They say how tight a turn will be. Later, he says, "Jiggy jiggy." This means the road zigzags.

FUN FACT

In races, turns are labeled 1–6. A wide turn is a 6. A very tight turn is a 1.

When rally racing, Pastrana often drives with a codriver who can guide him through difficult paths.

Pastrana turns sharply around a bend. The tire goes off the road slightly. It hits a small rock. They are both nervous. But the tire is okay. They keep speeding to the top of the mountain. It gets foggy as they go higher. It's hard to see. But they keep going.

Finally, they reach the top. It took 6 minutes and 20.47 seconds. They weren't racing. That means the record isn't official. But Pastrana knows he was the fastest. He knows it's a win.

CLIMB TO THE CLOUDS

Climb to the Clouds is a race. It's one of the oldest motorsport events in the United States. Drivers race up the Mount Washington Auto Road. The first race was in 1904. The winner took 24 minutes, 37 seconds. The race runs every three years.

FUN FACT
In 2017, Pastrana raced up Mount Washington again. His time was 5 minutes, 44 seconds.

The Mount Washington Auto Road features sharp turns, rocky edges, and sections without guardrails.

CHAPTER 2

RACING AROUND THE WORLD

The first-ever automobile race happened in 1894. It started in Paris, France. It ended 79 miles (127 km) to the northwest. The finish line was in Rouen, France. Twenty-one automobiles lined up. There were regular cars. There were even tractors and tricycles. The race was the start of something big.

Racing kept growing. In 1911, the prince of Monaco wanted to boost tourism. A race would attract visitors. He held the Monte Carlo Rally. It was the first race to use the word *rally*. Twenty-three racers competed. They started from eleven different cities. They could take any route they wanted. But they had to end in Monte Carlo.

Pierre lived in Monte Carlo. He and his father were in the town center. The race would come through here. Pierre asked, "Who do you think will be fastest?" His father told him it wasn't just about who's fastest. Design was important, too. The cars were driving a long way. The judges wanted to see how well they held up.

The crowd cheered. Pierre looked down the street. The first car was arriving! Racing was exciting. Pierre hoped he could go to another rally soon.

FUN FACT

Monaco is only 0.76 square miles (1.99 sq km).

The Monte Carlo Rally began in 1911 and is still held today.

RALLY CAR RACING

RECORDS

Tightest WRC rally finish

0.2 seconds, Jordan Rally, 2011

Oldest WRC event winner

Björn Waldegård, aged 46 years 155 days, Safari Rally Kenya, 1990

Most world titles

Sébastien Loeb, 9

Most WRC wins

Sébastien Loeb, 9

First woman to win a WRC event

Michèle Mouton, 1981

Fastest Climb to the Clouds run

Travis Pastrana, 2017, 5 min. 44.72 sec.

The World Rally Championship (WRC) takes place on many different roads with varying, sometimes dangerous, conditions.

The Monte Carlo Rally still happens today. It opens the World Rally Championship (WRC). Pierre's great-great-grandchildren can watch now! The Monte Carlo is a tough rally. Drivers race on narrow mountain roads. They face snow and ice. Winning is a big deal.

The WRC started in 1973. It's a series of rallies. Each rally takes place on public roads. The roads aren't usually paved. And they're closed off. The racers drive very fast. It can be dangerous.

Rallycross is a variation of rally racing that takes place on closed courses rather than public roads.

FUN FACT

Rally racing came to the X Games in 2006. Travis Pastrana won the first gold medal.

The WRC takes place every year. The series lasts all year. There are between twelve and sixteen races. They are in different cities. There are other rally series besides WRC. The United States has two of its own. Traditional rallies are done in stages. This means drivers race one at a time. They drive from one point to another. Whoever has the best time wins.

Rallycross is a **variation** of rally racing. It began in 1967. It takes place on closed courses, not public roads. Drivers compete head-to-head instead of in stages. Rallycross cars don't have to drive on public roads. That means they don't have to be **street legal**. They can be more powerful than regular rally cars.

CHAPTER 3

CARS AND CODRIVERS

"Left five, three hundred. Right three over **crest**. Five hundred. Left four, don't **cut**." Sophia reads the instructions aloud. The driver follows them exactly. Sophia is a rally codriver. Her brother Mason is the driver. They make a great team.

In US rally competitions, rally teams receive stage notes. These describe the route. Mason and Sophia came here yesterday. They did recce (RECK-ee). Recce is a practice round. They drove the route at slow speeds. During recce, Sophia changed some of the notes. She cut out information they didn't need.

TRANSLATING STAGE NOTES

Sophia's notes read "L5 300 R3/cr 500 L4 dc." Left five means a wide left turn. Then Mason has to drive straight for 300 yards (275 m). After that is a tight right turn (R3) over a crest. Then there's 500 yards (460 m) straight. Last is a medium left turn (L4). But a tree is inside. Mason can't cut the turn. The "dc" in Sophia's notes stands for "don't cut."

In practice rounds, rally drivers and their codrivers write or update their stage notes to prepare for the official race.

FUN FACT

In European competitions, codrivers have to write all their own notes.

Sophia wears the same safety gear as her brother. They both wear helmets. They wear **flame-retardant** suits. The car has special gear, too. It has a safety cage. This protects them if the car rolls. Rally races are run on closed sections of public roads. But drivers use regular roads to get between stages. This means rally cars have to be street legal. They need working lights and insurance. They need everything regular cars have.

Rally cars have roll cages to protect the driver and codriver in case the car flips or rolls.

THE RALLY CAR

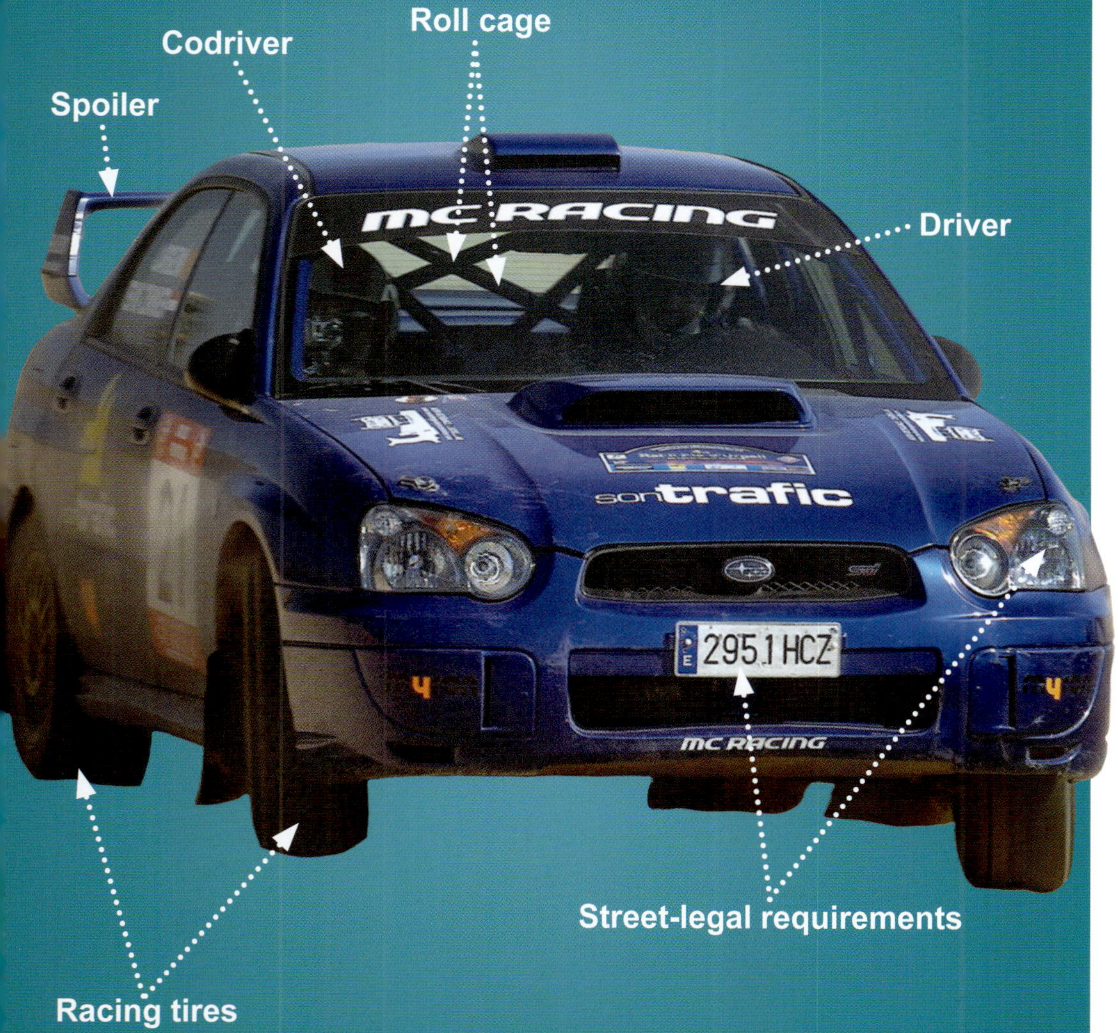

Many people enjoy rally car racing.

Rally cars are based on street cars. They have to stay as similar as possible. Mason drives a Ford Fiesta. It's different from ones on the street. It looks similar on the outside. But the inside is different. There's more than just the safety cage. The car has fixed seats. And it doesn't have back seats. It also has a more powerful engine. The brakes are bigger. The car even has a rubber fuel tank. Rubber is less likely to break in a crash. This car is meant just for racing.

Rally cars are similar to street cars because they have to be street legal, but they have many differences on the inside.

CHAPTER 4

Sébastien Loeb has had an impressive rally racing career.

FUN FACT
Sébastien Loeb did a backflip on the podium in 2004.

FAMOUS RALLY DRIVERS

Sébastien Loeb began his athletic career as a gymnast. He won five gold medals in the French Gymnastics Championships. He was only fifteen. But in 1995, he switched gears. He started rally racing. He first competed in the WRC in 2002. He won his first title in 2004. He went on to win nine world titles. He's also won seventy-nine WRC races. The person behind him won forty-four. Loeb has a record-breaking career. It earned him the nickname "Le Patron." That means "the boss" in French.

In 1981, Michèle Mouton was the only female racer in the WRC. Journalists treated her differently. Other racers thought she was a publicity stunt. But she proved herself.

She showed that she deserved to be there. She was the first woman to win a WRC event. It was the 1981 Sanremo rally. She won three more rallies the next year.

Michèle Mouton, right, proved that women could race with men by winning rally after rally.

Mouton retired from racing in 1986. But she's still involved with the sport. The International Automobile Federation sets the rules for car racing. It created a Women in Motorsport Commission. That was in 2009. Mouton was elected president. She works with **ambassadors**. They help get more girls and women racing.

Rally racing has come a long way since the Monte Carlo Rally in 1911. As technology changes, so does the sport. It's exciting to think about what the future holds.

Mouton, third from left, stays involved with rally car racing through the Women in Motorsport Commission.

THREE STARS OF
RALLY CAR RACING

TRAVIS PASTRANA

Travis Pastrana is a famous American motorsport athlete. He's won four Rally America championships. He's raced in NASCAR. He also competes in freestyle motocross. At the 2011 X Games, Pastrana broke his foot and ankle doing freestyle motocross.

SÉBASTIEN LOEB

Sébastien Loeb is one of the greatest rally drivers of all time. He won gold in rallycross at the 2012 X Games. He was awarded the French Legion of Honor in 2009. This is the highest honor given by the French government.

MICHÈLE MOUTON

By 2019, Michèle Mouton was still the only woman to win a WRC event. And she's won four. She raced in an Audi Quattro. She won the difficult Pikes Peak International Hill Climb in 1984. She won again in 1985. That time, she set a new record.

BEYOND THE BOOK

After reading the book, it's time to think about what you learned. Try the following exercises to jumpstart your ideas.

THINK

THAT'S NEWS TO ME. Sébastien Loeb won his first WRC title in 2004. How might news sources be able to fill in more detail about this event? What new information could you find in news articles? Where could you go to find those sources?

CREATE

PRIMARY SOURCES. A primary source is a document that provides a first-hand account of an event, such as a photograph, video, or interview. Make a list of different primary sources you might be able to find about rally car racing. What new information might you learn from these sources?

SHARE

SUM IT UP. Write one paragraph summarizing the important points from this book. Make sure it's in your own words. Don't just copy the text. Then share the paragraph with a classmate. Does your classmate have any comments about the summary or any additional questions about rally car racing?

GROW

REAL-LIFE RESEARCH. What real-world places could you visit to learn more about rally car racing? What other things could you learn while you were there?

RESEARCH NINJA

Visit *www.ninjaresearcher.com/0677* to learn how to take your research skills and book report writing to the next level!

RESEARCH

DIGITAL LITERACY TOOLS

SEARCH LIKE A PRO
Learn about how to use search engines to find useful websites.

FACT OR FAKE?
Discover how you can tell a trusted website from an untrustworthy resource.

TEXT DETECTIVE
Explore how to zero in on the information you need most.

SHOW YOUR WORK
Research responsibly—learn how to cite sources.

WRITE

GET TO THE POINT
Learn how to express your main ideas.

PLAN OF ATTACK
Learn prewriting exercises and create an outline.

DOWNLOADABLE REPORT FORMS

FURTHER RESOURCES

BOOKS

Bowman, Chris. *Rally Car Racing*. Bellwether Media, 2016.

Howell, Brian. *Rally Car Racing: Tearing It Up*. Lerner Publications Company, 2014.

Von Finn, Denny. *Rally Cars*. Bellwether Media, 2009.

WEBSITES

FACTSURFER

Factsurfer.com gives you a safe, fun way to find more information.

1. Go to www.factsurfer.com.
2. Enter "Rally Car Racing" into the search box and click 🔍.
3. Select your book cover to see a list of related websites.

GLOSSARY

ambassadors: Ambassadors are people who represent a government or organization. Women in Motorsport ambassadors go around the world to try to get girls interested in racing.

communicate: To communicate means to talk to and understand one another. Drivers and codrivers have to communicate well to finish the race.

crest: A crest is the top of a hill. Codrivers tell drivers when a crest is coming up and help them drive through whatever is behind it.

cut: To cut a corner means to drive off the road to get through the corner faster. Sophia tells Mason not to cut the corner because there's a tree.

flame retardant: Something that is flame retardant does not catch fire easily. Rally drivers and codrivers wear flame-retardant suits to protect them.

street legal: A car that is street legal meets the standards to be driven on public roads. Because rally cars drive on public roads, they need things like headlights and turn signals to be street legal.

variation: A variation is a slightly different version of something else. Rallycross is a variation of rally racing.

INDEX

PHOTO CREDITS

The images in this book are reproduced through the courtesy of: Ivan Garcia/Shutterstock Images, front cover (car), pp. 22–23; ESOlex/Shutterstock Images, front cover (road); freelanceartist/Shutterstock Images, front cover (background); EvrenKalinbacak/Shutterstock Images, pp. 3, 20; Jon Bilous/Shutterstock Images, p. 4; action sports/Shutterstock Images, pp. 4–5; Daniel Phillip/Shutterstock Images, pp. 6–7; Jim Cole/AP Images, p. 8; Photawa/iStockphoto, p. 9; Branger/Roger Viollet/Getty Images, pp. 10–11; Red Line Editorial, pp. 12, 27; Corepics VOF/Shutterstock Images, p. 13; betto rodrigues/Shutterstock Images, pp. 14–15, 17 (bottom); Manamana/Shutterstock Images, p. 17 (top); ermess/Shutterstock Images, p. 18; Rodrigo Garrido/Shutterstock Images, pp. 19, 27 (middle); Jon Ingall/Shutterstock Images, p. 21; cristiano barni/Shutterstock Images, p. 23; Saris/AP Images, pp. 24–25; Alexander Sandvoss/picture-alliance/dpa/AP Images, p. 26; David Blair/Cal Sport Media/AP Images, p. 27 (top); Langevin/AP Images, p. 27 (bottom); Taras Vyshnya/Shutterstock Images, p. 30.

ABOUT THE AUTHOR

K. A. Hale is a writer and editor from Minnesota. She enjoys reading, writing, and playing with her dog.